THIS HOPE JOURNAL BELONGS TO:

_____

Copyright © 2024 by Candice Hayes

All rights reserved. This book or any portion thereof may not be reproduced or used in any manner whatsoever without the express written permission of the publisher except for the use of brief quotations in a book review.

Limits of Liability and Disclaimer of Warranty

The author and publisher shall not be liable for your misuse of this material. This journal is strictly for writing purposes. The author and publisher do not guarantee anyone using this journal, writing, techniques, suggestions, tips, ideas, or strategies will become successful. The author and publisher shall have neither liability nor responsibility to anyone with respect to any loss or damage caused, or alleged to be caused, directly or indirectly by the information contained in this book. Views expressed in this publication do not necessarily reflect the views of the publisher.

Printed in the United States of America
Keen Vision Publishing, LLC
www.publishwithKVP.com
ISBN: 978-1-955316-65-1

Hello,

Life throws challenges at us that we never anticipate. For me, the founder of Candy's Candles, one of those challenges came in the form of my youngest son's mental health crisis. The struggle with my son's mental health was long, silent, and weighed heavy on our family for years. Yet, through it all, two things kept me going: my faith and the art of candle-making. In 2016, just two weeks before my daughter's wedding, our world was shaken. Our youngest son had a psychotic break. This was a challenge we kept private, a pain we dealt with in the silence of our home. The rollercoaster of emotions became our life, filled with ups and downs dictated by medical treatments and hospital visits. Then came a day that changed everything—a day that came dangerously close to becoming a tragic ending. The room was quiet; my son was quieter. An uneasy feeling gripped me, compelling me to alter my schedule. I abandoned my plans and started making candles, my therapy. That feeling led me to my son's room, where I found him in a critical state, and my immediate actions saved his life.

That traumatic experience sparked a realization: What do other parents like me who suffer in silence do to relieve stress? Who cares for the caretaker?

How are others who are dealing with overwhelming stress managing time for self-care? So, I decided it was time to break the silence and offer something that signifies resilience, faith, and, above all, hope: The Hope Candle & The Hope Journal.

This *Hope Journal* was designed for people so bogged down by life's challenges that they never have a moment to check in on themselves. *The Hope Journal* is your time to breathe, process, reflect, and heal. There are three sections of journaling writing prompts, Self-Care, Challenges, and Feelings. You can use these prompts to guide your writing or write whatever you feel. The key is to take intentional time to express yourself on paper. Studies show that journaling, when done consistently, can be healing, refreshing, and renewing. I hope that you enjoy adding journaling with *The Hope Journal* to your self-care routine.

Candice Hayes
Owner of Candy's Candles
facebook: Candice H. Hayes & Conversation with Candice
instagram: @candyscandlescollection
website: www.conversationwithcandice.com
www.candyscandles.com

SELF-GUIDED
Journaling Prompts

SELF-CARE

- What does setting boundaries mean to you? With who and when do you experience difficulty setting boundaries?
- When faced with family crisis, what are things that help you maintain your strength?
- What are some weekly things you do that will impact your mental well-being?
- What concerns keep you from resting well at night?
- How can you celebrate yourself today? What would you celebrate?
- What signs tell you that you are close to burnout? What do you do when those signs arise? How can you better prevent burnout in the future?
- What are 10 words you would use to describe who you are now. What are 10 words you would like to describe yourself in the future?
- List 5 things you will say no to. List 5 things you will say yes to. Why are you making these adjustments in your life?
- What does unconditional love for self look like to you?
- What are your life values? Are you living in alignment with those values? What adjustments are necessary?

SELF-GUIDED
Journaling Prompts

FEELINGS

- What emotions are you struggling with at this moment?
- Is there a time you felt overwhelmed? What were your ways to overcome it?
- Write about a time you had to suppress your feelings or emotions to help someone else?
- If you had to write a letter to yourself during a very challenging time, what would be some comforting words to give?
- Write about a moment you felt the most powerful.
- Do you struggle with being out of control? What feelings surface when you aren't in control of your circumstances?
- What negative feelings surface when you put yourself first? What positive feelings surface?
- How do you feel about your life? What would you change?
- Who are you struggling to forgive? What are you struggling to forgive yourself for?
- Write about a moment you felt proud of yourself.
- Write about a time someone did something that hurt your feelings. How did you respond? What did that moment teach you about yourself?
- Make a list of 30 things that makes you smile.

SELF-GUIDED
Journaling Prompts

CHALLENGES

- What has been an obstacle in your life that turned out to be the greatest accomplishment that can be shared with others?
- What are some failures that's developed your growth into who you are today?
- What is one of your most greatest challenges to overcome? What did you learn about yourself?
- What can you do today that you couldn't do a year ago? What feelings surface when you think about that?
- What do you typically do when you are faced with a challenge?
- How do you talk to yourself when you make a mistake? How do you talk to others when they make a mistake? Is there a difference?
- Write about a goal you have been working on. What challenges have you faced?
- Write about opportunities that surfaced from challenges you've endured.
- What makes you feel inspired when you are dealing with difficulties?
- Who is someone you would like to treat better or treat you better? What challenging conversations need to take place? How do you feel about having those conversations?

www.ingramcontent.com/pod-product-compliance
Lightning Source LLC
Chambersburg PA
CBHW042027050526
44107CB00103B/729